Ron Ransom's Favorite Santas for Carvers

D1091760

Ron Ransom

Schiffer Publishing Ltd

4880 Lower Valley Road, Atglen, PA 19310 USA

Dedication

To the Woodchuck Carving Club of Reno, Nevada. And to my newest grandson, David, and my step granddaughter, Katie.

Copyright © 2006 by Ron Ransom
Library of Congress Control Number: 2005931372

Designed by Joseph M. Riggio Jr.
Type set in Benguiat Bk BT/Humanist 521 BT

ISBN: 0-7643-2362-8
Printed in China

Published by Schiffer Publishing Ltd.
4880 Lower Valley Road
Atglen, PA 19310
Phone: (610) 593-1777; Fax: (610) 593-2002
E-mail: Info@schifferbooks.com

For the largest selection of fine reference books on this and related subjects, please visit our web site at
www.schifferbooks.com
We are always looking for people to write books on new and related subjects. If you have an idea for a book please contact us at the above address.

This book may be purchased from the publisher.
Include $3.95 for shipping.
Please try your bookstore first.
You may write for a free catalog.

In Europe, Schiffer books are distributed by
Bushwood Books
6 Marksbury Ave.
Kew Gardens
Surrey TW9 4JF England
Phone: 44 (0) 20 8392-8585; Fax: 44 (0) 20 8392-9876
E-mail: info@bushwoodbooks.co.uk
Free postage in the U.K., Europe; air mail at cost.

Foreword

Imagine you are starting a woodcarving club from scratch. No experienced carvers, a blank slate to start writing on. You want to get your club off to a good start with an instructor and a project that will instill enthusiasm and confidence in the new students, and leave them with a carving they can be proud of.

This was the situation we found ourselves in when we decided to start a woodcarving group in Reno, Nevada. And boy did we hit the jackpot when we asked Ron Ransom to come and be our inaugural instructor.

I had only met Ron by telephone, when I bought one of his original Santas as a Christmas gift. He graciously accepted our invitation to come to Reno. Ron is a tremendous instructor. His projects are as simple as you want them to be, and yet can be subtle and challenging to experienced carvers who want to give them a little variation. All of our carvers enthusiastically embraced the hobby after spending a weekend of woodcarving with Ron. And our club has been growing ever since.

My wife, Teri, and I also had the privilege of hosting Ron and Evelyn and showing them around the greater Reno area. We shopped for antiques, saw the sights, ate, and laughed the entire time they were here. Ron is an accomplished storyteller, cartoonist, woodcarver, companion, and friend. We feel like we've known them both forever.

I hope you enjoy this book as much as I have enjoyed carving from Ron's patterns over the years. Make your carvings as simple or as complicated as you wish – this is possible with Ron's designs, and it is what makes his designs unique.

And above all, as Ron would say: Have fun!

—Paul Volpp
Reno Woodchucks Woodcarving Club
Reno, Nevada
December 4, 2004

Contents

Introduction

The letters I have received from people who have used my books have asked for additional ideas. For the experienced carver, a book of drawings of patterns are well and good. The less experienced carvers need a little more help. I have hopefully put this book together for both types. The more experienced can run with these ideas and the others will have the added help they need.

I have been teaching at The John C. Campbell Folk School in Brasstown, North Carolina, since 1997. I teach Santa carving for a week and there are at least twelve other classes going on at the same time, which includes everything from blacksmithing to candle making. Each class has new carvers, experienced carvers, and for the first time last year I had a blind carver. It is impossible to know ahead of time the skill level of these students. After the first year, I decided to have everyone work with the same blank and I gave them different ideas about objects for the Santa to be holding. If they didn't like what I showed them, they could choose to use an idea of their own (within reason). Janis, one of my Quarterly Tax Club members, wanted something special for her daughter, who was graduating from Medical School. She had one of her Santas holding an enema bag. I am using the same method for this book and will show some of the favorites from several years of teaching at the school.

A letter from a student:

After buying a vacation home in the North Georgia Mountains, we discovered the unexpected treasure of the John C. Campbell Folk School in Brasstown, North Carolina. My husband and I gave my mother and sister gift certificates to take a weeklong course at the Folk School. My sister jumped on the opportunity to take woodcarving from our beloved friend, Ron Ransom. My Mom and I planned to take jewelry making as I was perfectly happy being a Ransom collector! Since the jewelry class was full, we had to choose between blacksmithing or Ron's woodcarving class. I promised my Mom that Ron's wonderful sense of humor and kind manner would make any class enjoyable. I quickly prayed for the good Lord to give me enough talent so not to spoil the week for my sister and we signed up for a week of making Old World Santas.

Long story short, it was a delightful week with my family. Ron taught and helped us make darling Santas, and I fell in love with carving! Like any addict, I have enjoyed an unquenchable desire to learn more, try new styles, and buy tools! I immediately signed up for another carving class at the Folk School and during the last five years have taken classes with John Burke, Vic Hood, Wayne Shinlever, Tom Wolfe, Jerry King, Jim Barton, Roy Hellman, and many classes with the Folk School's Resident Carver, Helen Gibson. As a hobby carver, I carve just for the fun of it. Lately, I have been studying nativity figures with Helen Gibson and also have fallen in love with mallet-style carving woodspirits and large format pieces. I will be forever grateful to Ron for introducing me to the wonderful world of carving and still find carving his Santas the most fun of all!

—Kimberly Maynard
February 2005

If you would like to receive a catalog from the school, call 1-800-FOLK-SCH or at www.folkschool.org on the web. I will answer any reasonable questions, provided you send a self addressed stamped envelope along with your questions to:

Ron Ransom
3651 Hickory Ridge Court
Marietta, GA 30066

The painting on my Santa figures is well done by Scott Ransom.

Most Asked Questions

Q. How long does it take to do a Santa?

A. That's a tough one. I've done a hundred or so and I know what needs to come off and I carve pretty fast. It took two days to carve the unpainted Santas shown in this book. To save time, I had my son, Scott, paint the finished examples for me before I came to Pennsylvania. Typically, in my classes at John C. Campbell, it takes a day to have a Santa ready for painting. An experienced carver will generally take less time and a novice may take more. Some "detail oriented" carvers have a difficult time knowing when they are finished.

Q. What kind of wood do you use?

A. I use basswood that I purchase from Heinecke Wood Products in Wisconsin. They can be reached by phone at (715) 822-8642. I have my wood cut 1 3/4 inches thick.

Q. Is it possible to make a living carving Santas?

A. If you live in a cave and hunt and fish for food you probably could. Seriously, several carvers who started carving from my first book do okay. The carvers I've heard from are Nancy Goff, Deborah Call, Marcia Berkall, David Francis, and Al Longo. You probably can find them on the internet. If not, write to me at the address at the front of the book.

Q. You always show Ceramcoat™ paint by Delta in your books. Why?

A. I started using Ceramcoat™ with my first carvings and I like it. I know it will always give me the results I want.

Q. It seems like every book you do you suggest a new antiquing product. What's the deal?

A. In my first book I suggested Griffin Bark™ Brown Shoe Polish. I don't know if they went out of business, but nobody could find it. One type of antiquing I suggested would take the paint off if you didn't follow the instructions. Finally, I found a product from Delta that works. It is Antiquing Gel™ and I prefer Dark Brown. I called before I did my latest book and they assured me they planned to be in business for a long time.

Q. How much should I ask for my Santas?

A. This too is a tough one. I would visit craft shows or check in shops that sell Santas. Compare what you're doing with other carvers' work.

Santa Patterns

Ron Ranson

RonRansom

Ron Ransom

Carving & Painting Santas

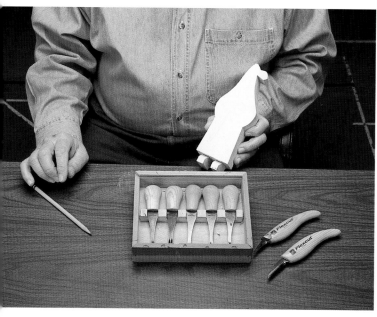

These are the basic tools we use on this series of Santas. They are Flexcut™ knives, which are good for new and old carvers alike. They come sharp and stay sharp with just a little tender loving care. We will be using the same pattern on all but two Santas, with a little variation for the flag holding Santa. You will see the many variations you can create with the face, even using the same pattern each time. I'll start with the golfer because he's one of my best sellers and he is relatively simple for new carvers.

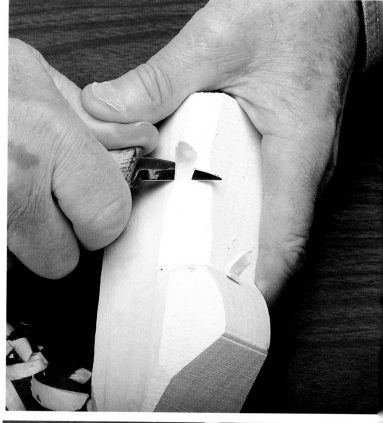

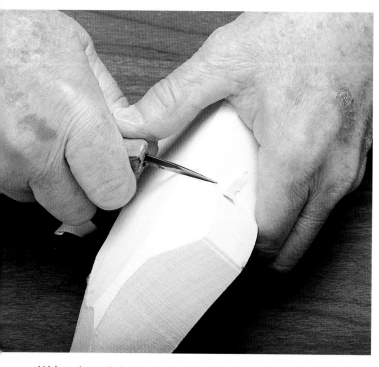

We're taking a little V cut out of the left elbow area on Santa's back. Notice I'm pushing with my left thumb on top of my right thumb.

Rounding the back side. When I'm carving toward myself, I'm using my thumb to brace the knife for greater control.

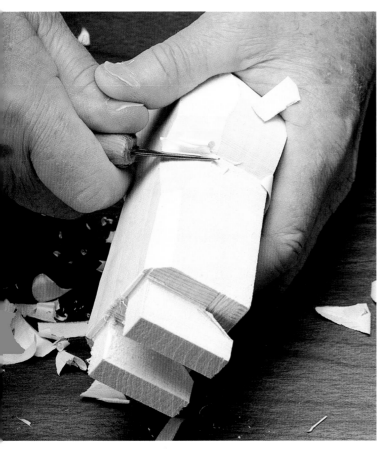

Repeat this process on the right.

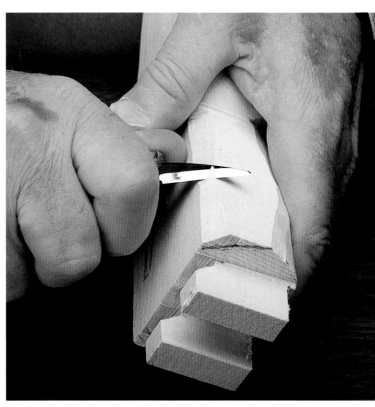

Starting on the left side, begin rounding to the pencil mark. The grain in basswood is very subtle so be very careful not to take chunks off.

You may want to draw in an oval on the bottom of the robe to make sure you get the roundness that I like.

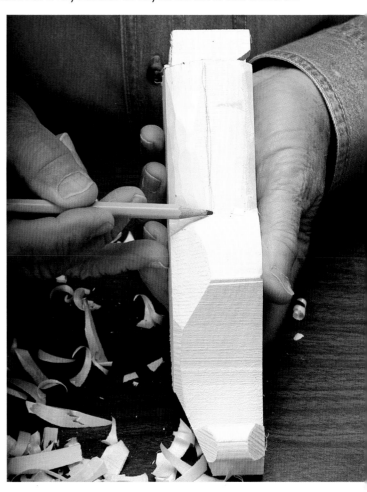

You may want to draw a line down the center and carve to that centerline. Without this line to carve to, your robe will get narrower than you like.

Repeating this rounding on the right.

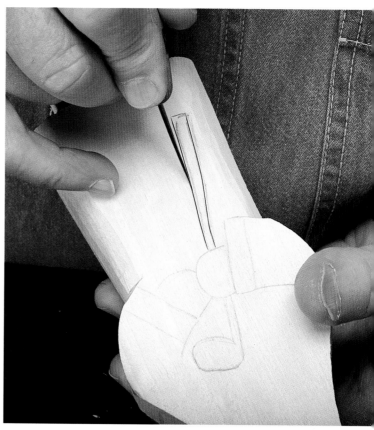

To make sure I don't take too much away from the golf club shaft, I'm incising the lines of the shaft and then the entire golf club.

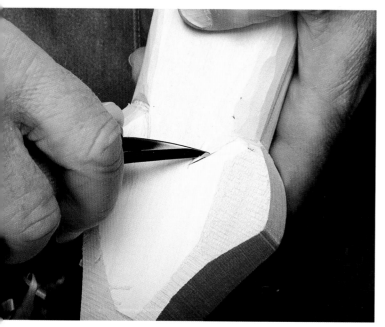

Make a little V cut on the back of the arm to give it shape.

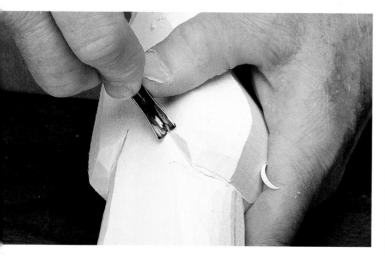

To give you a choice, I'm giving the back of the other arm its shape with a V gouge. Either method will work fine.

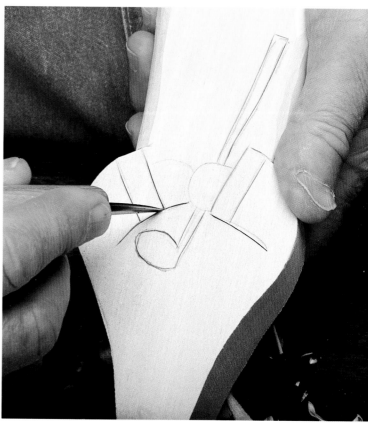

I am deeply incising all the other pencil lines.

Round the front of the right arm.

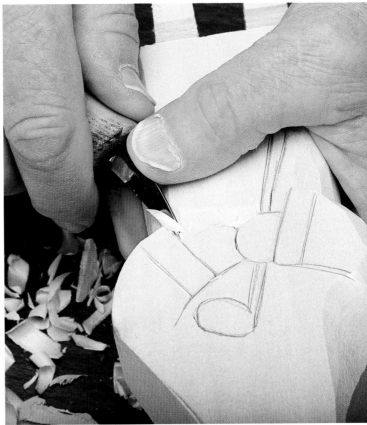

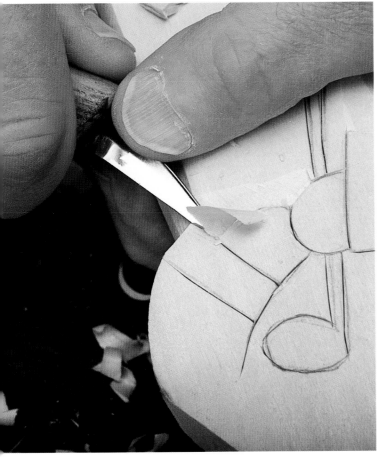

Cutting out around the base of the arm, where the glove goes into the sleeve.

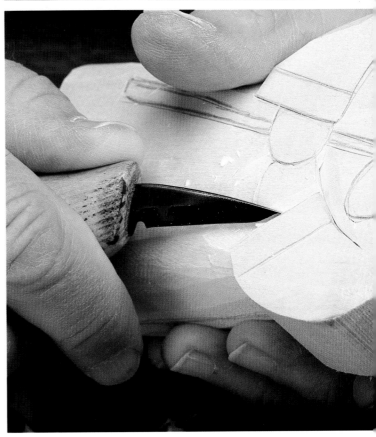

Incise a little V cut to show the hand going into the sleeve.

Incising around the golf club shaft so the shaft will stick out.

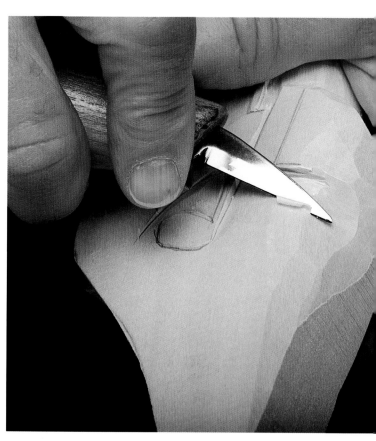

Rounding the shoulder area, getting ready to start on the face.

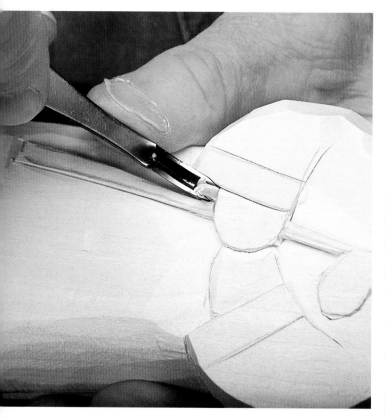

I'm using a small gouge to get in a tight spot between the club shaft and the hand. I don't encourage new carvers to buy a whole lot of equipment before they decide if they enjoy carving. Everything I have done can be done with a knife.

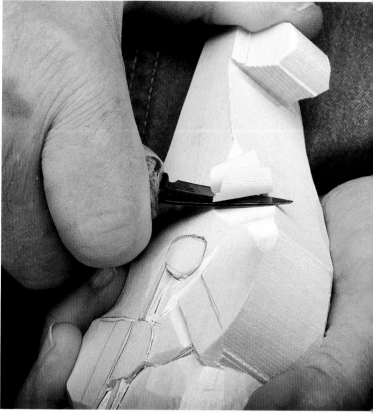

Doing the same on the other side. On this side I find the carving easier if I brace my thumb against the top of Santa's hood and carefully draw the knife toward me.

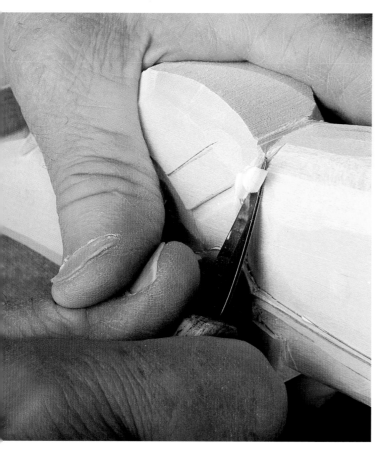

Rounding the front of the shoulder.

As you remember from my first book, I caution new carvers against leaving their Santa's too square. Rounding the front of the robe up to the arm.

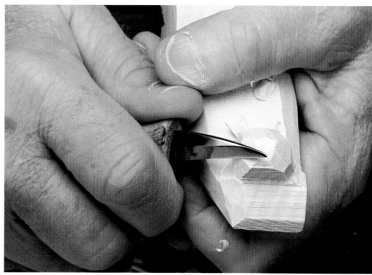

Rounding the ball on Santa's hat.

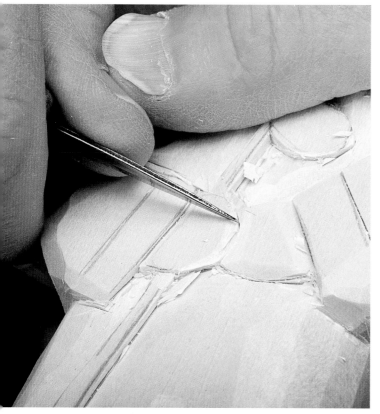

The left hand is going under the right hand. Rounding the hand.

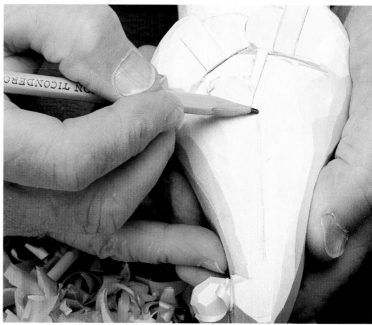

Before I start on the face, I draw a centerline.

Start rounding to that centerline in the area of the face and hat.

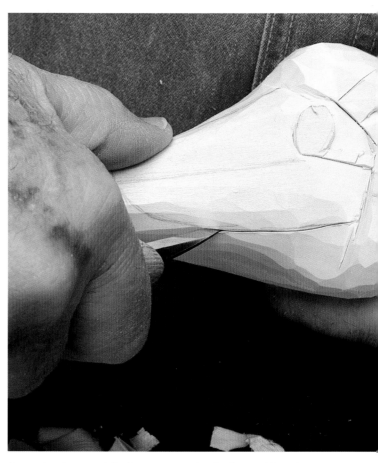

Incise deeply around the line we put in for the face and beard.

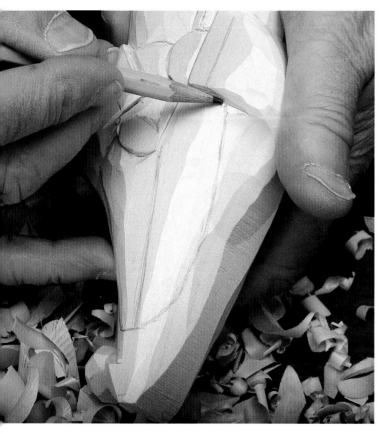

This is the outline for the face and the beard.

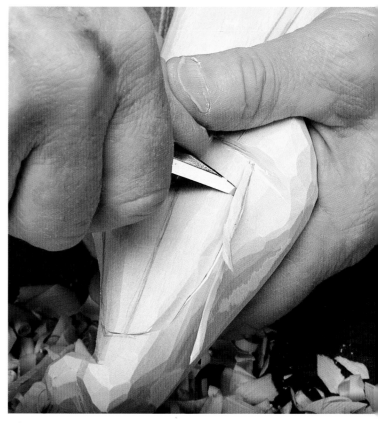

Come back around at an angle and cut into the incised line around the face.

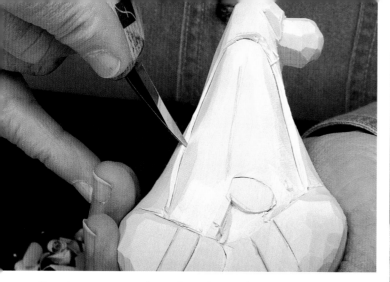

I've taken excess wood away from the area I incised around the face to separate the face from the hood.

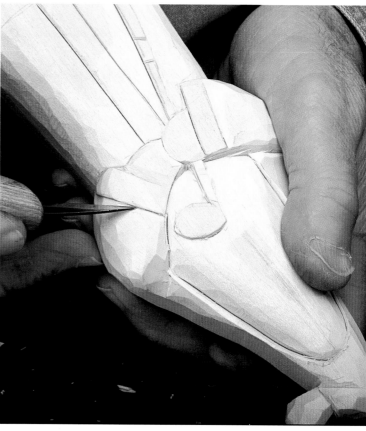

Cleaning around the cuffs, cutting away from the sleeve to make the cuff stand out.

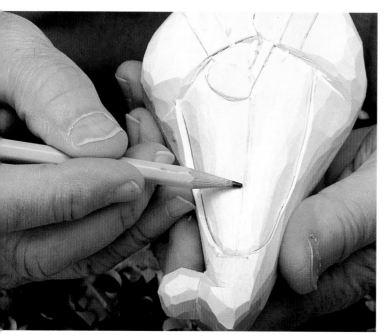

Round up to the centerline to get the shape of an egg. Do not cut the centerline away.

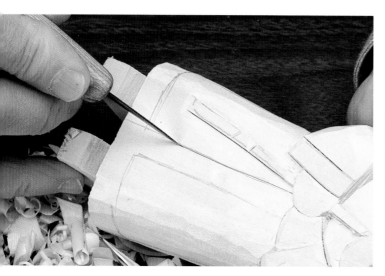

Incise the lines for all the fur around the coat and cuffs.

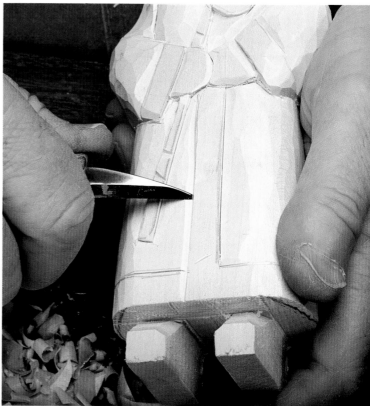

Cutting in at an angle to cut away the coat from the fur down the front and around the back.

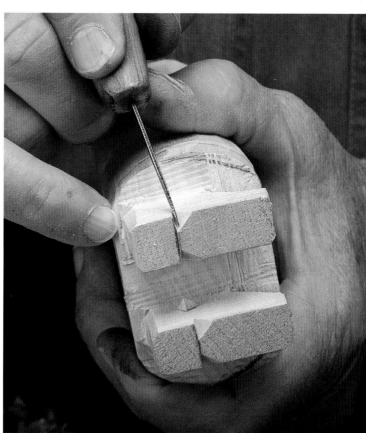

Notch the corners of the heel to separate it from the boot. Notch both the inside and outside of each boot. If you were to cut all the way across you might weaken the heel and end up cutting it off.

Rounding the shoes a bit.

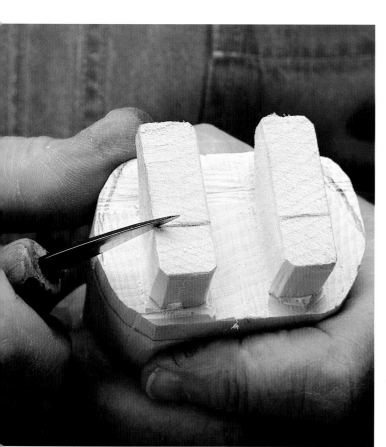

I've drawn a line to indicate the location of the heel. Incise the line.

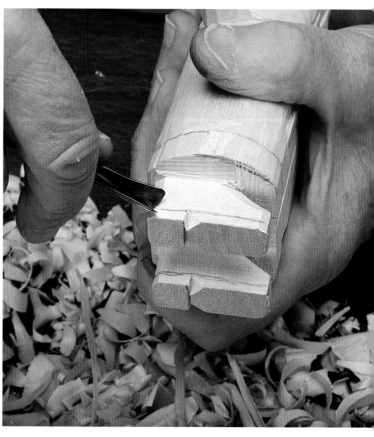

Draw a line all the way around the boot for the soles.

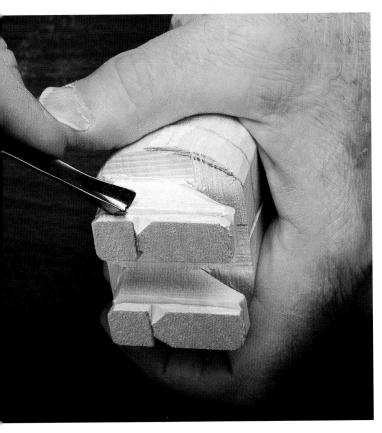

Create your boot soles with the V gouge. It can be done with a knife, but it is easier with the V gouge.

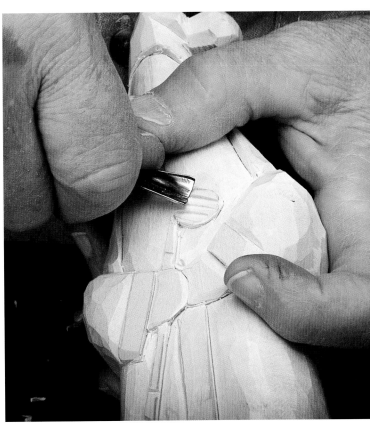

Using a V gouge, put some grooves in the club's head. This is a right-hander's club. Turn the head to the left for a left-hander's club.

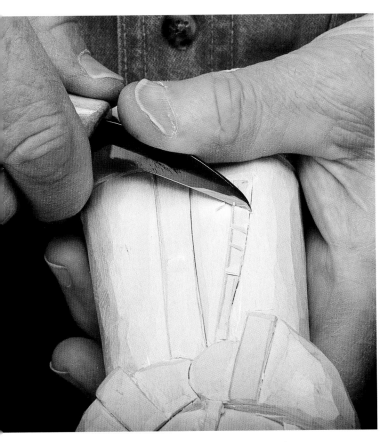

Using your knife, make little gouges for the golf club's grip.

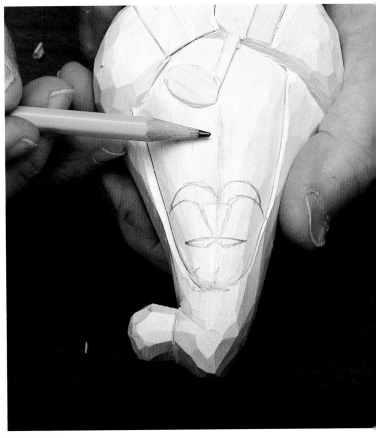

Draw in your centerline again and draw in the face.

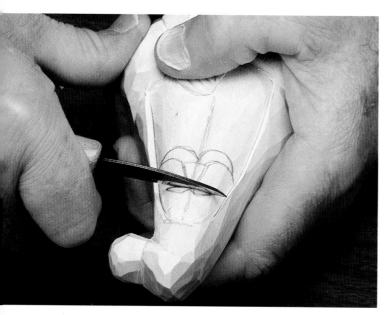

Cut a deep line across the eyes.

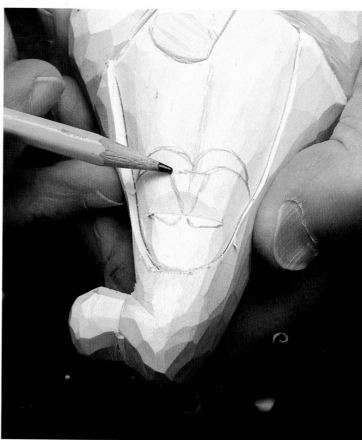

I've redrawn the nose and the eyebrows.

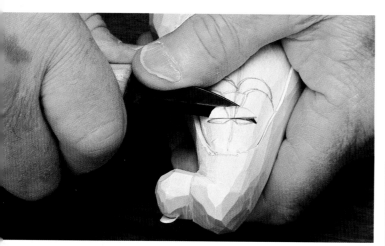

Come in at an angle up to the eye line you just put in to remove excess wood below the eyebrows.

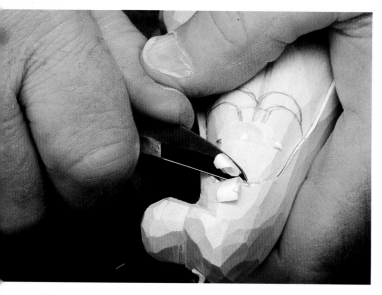

Cutting away excess wood from the forehead up to the hood. This will give the nose more prominence.

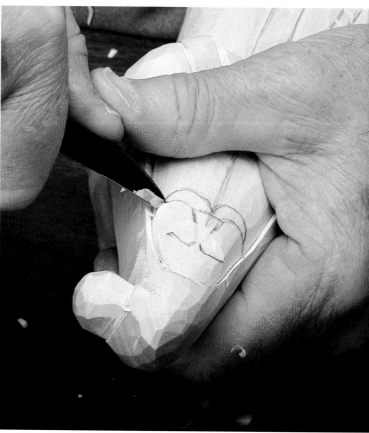

Incise around the nose, mustache, and cheeks.

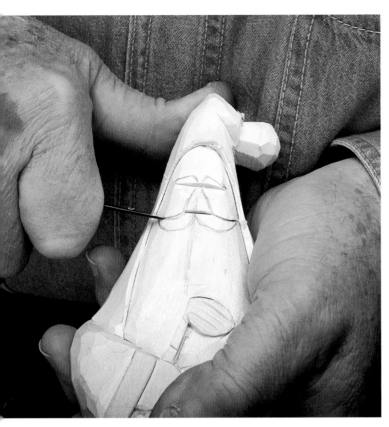

I've turned the Santa over to carve the other side of the cheek and mustache. It feels more natural that way.

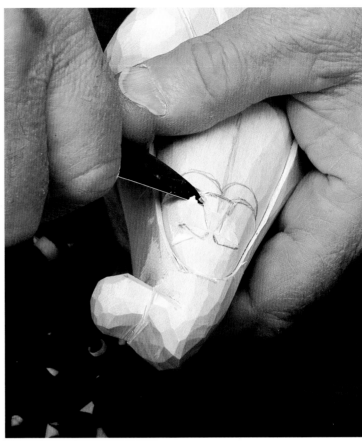

Come in at an angle and take out a piece along each side of the nose.

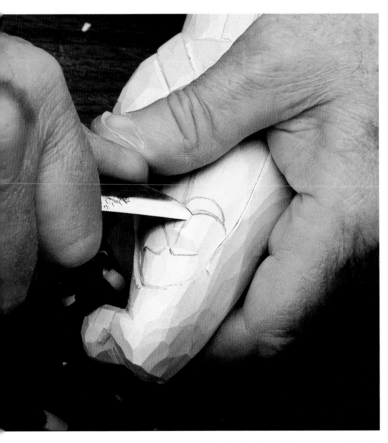

Angle the blade when you carve along both sides of the nose so the nose will have some shape.

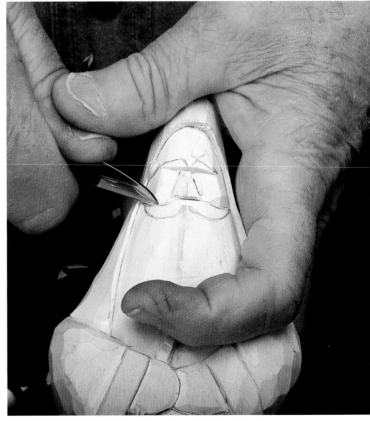

Round the cheek into the mustache – the rounder, the better.

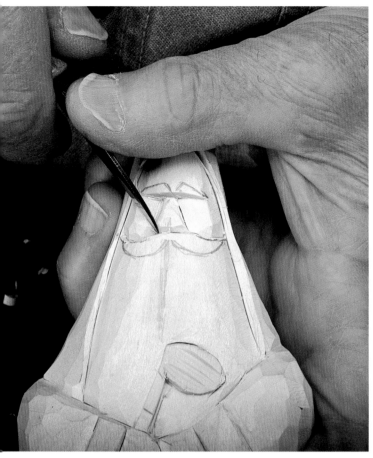

Come back and trim a little corner off the outer edge of each side of the nose.

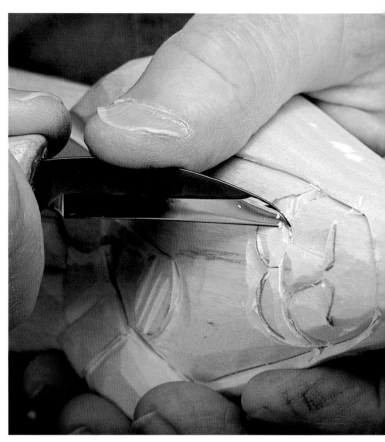

Blend the top of the mustache into the cheek.

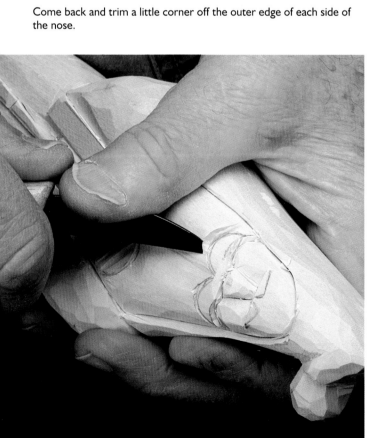

Incise around both sides of the mustache.

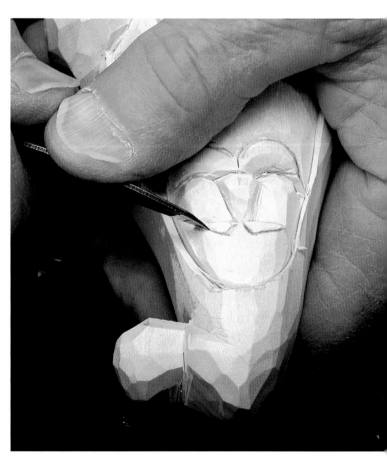

Incise around both eyebrows.

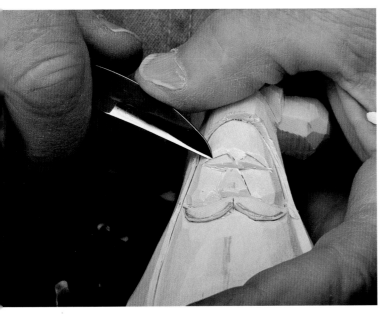

Carefully angle in to the incised line at the top of the eyebrow. Be careful when carving this line or the eyebrow will pop off.

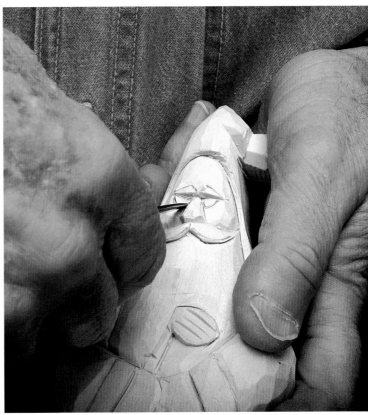

Do the same thing on the other side of the eye. Stick the blade in deep.

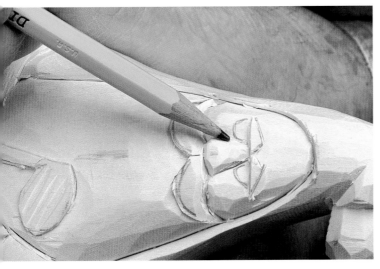

Draw in the eye, which is actually half a circle.

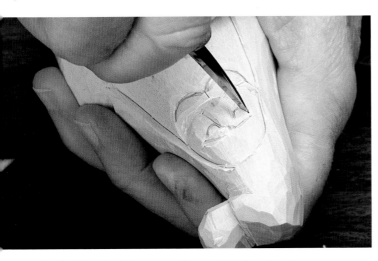

On the left side of the eye, stick your blade in rather deep.

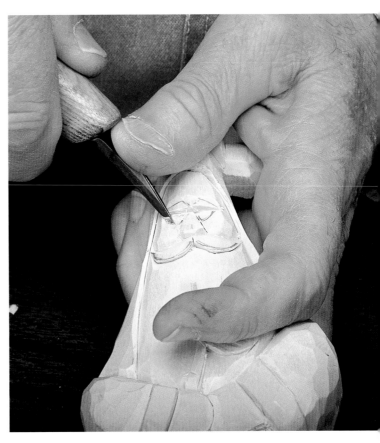

Round the eye down into the cheek. Repeat these steps on the other eye.

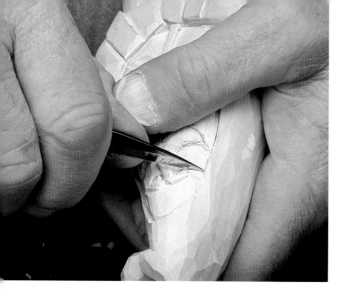

Cut in little laugh lines around the eyes.

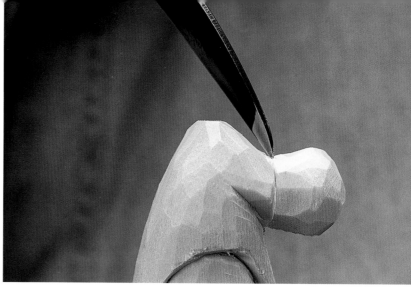

Round down the ball on the hood. If you don't want to have a ball on Santa's hat, don't carve one. Honestly, I carve the ball to have a place to hang a price tag.

The laugh lines are in place.

Paint the Santa with Tompte Red, Flesh Tone, White, Black, Dark Brown antiquing gel … and this is important, on each Santa after you are finished painting and it is dry, spray it with Semi Gloss Deft Clear Wood Finish™. After it is antiqued with the antiquing gel and dry, spray another light coat of Deft on it. The drying process can be encouraged with a hairdryer.

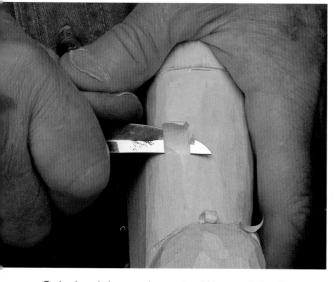

Go back and clean up the carving. I like to call this cleaning up the "wood boogers" in class.

Here's the back view.

Incise the line separating the arm from the body.

This is a Santa holding a snowman. I have taken away some of the waste wood with the Foredom™ tool to save time.

Cleaning out between the arm and the robe, giving it a little definition with a V gouge.

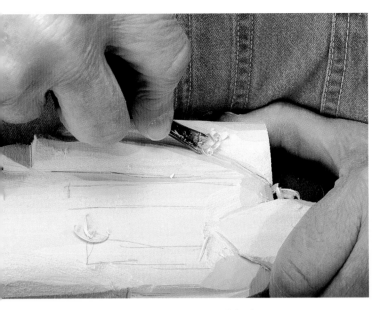

Repeat this process between the arm and the bag.

Repeat this process on the back of the bag.

Cleaning out along the back of the arm with the V gouge.

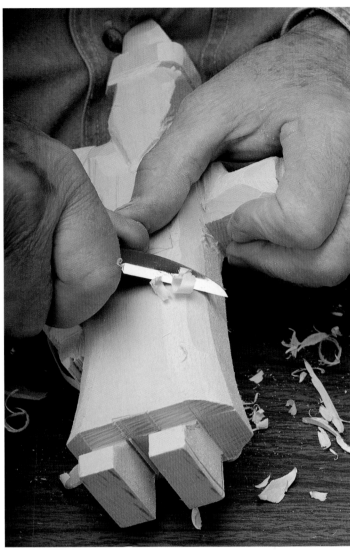

Rounding down the front of the robe with a knife.

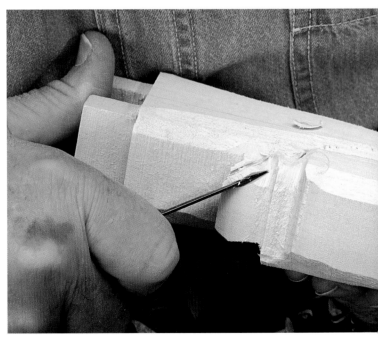

Shaping the hand.

Use the V gouge to shape the thumb. If you don't have a V gouge, a knife will work fine.

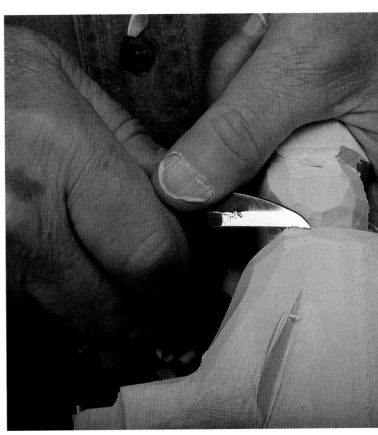

Continuing to round the back of the hair.

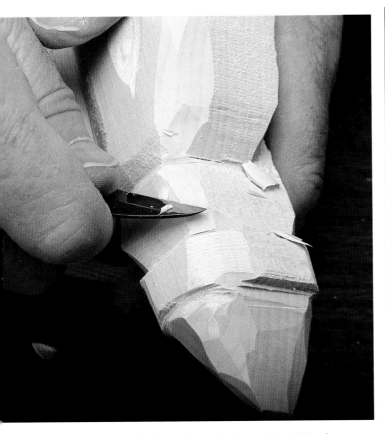

I'm starting to shape the hair and beard with my "big old" knife.

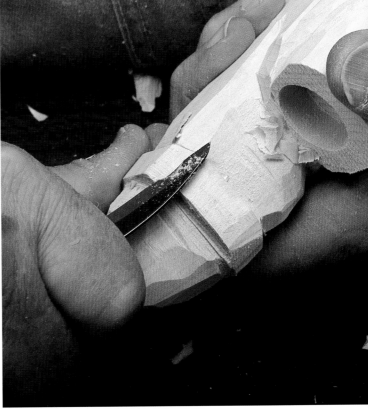

Rounding the fur on the cap.

Place the centerline on the face.

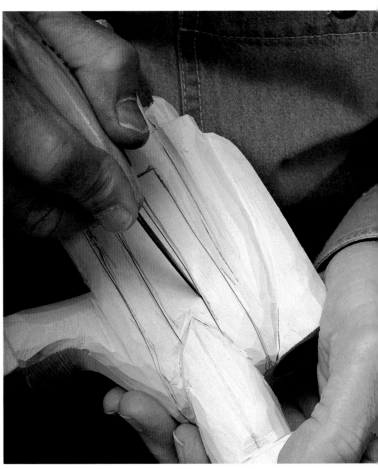

Incising around the scarf.

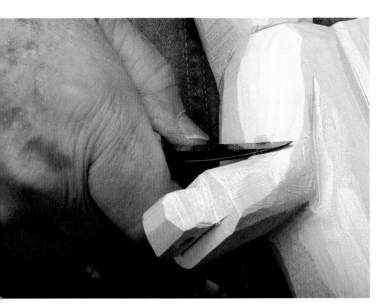

Continuing to round the arm.

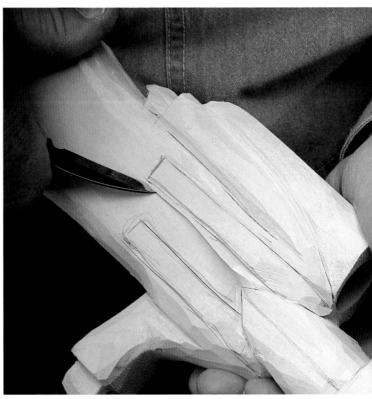

Cut back in at a steep angle to the incised scarf lines, cutting away the coat from the scarf.

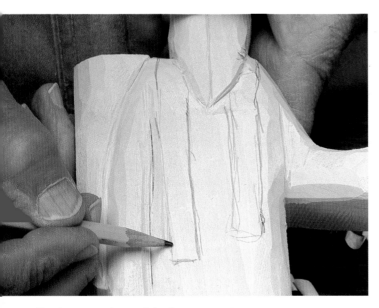

I'm drawing in the scarf this Santa is wearing.

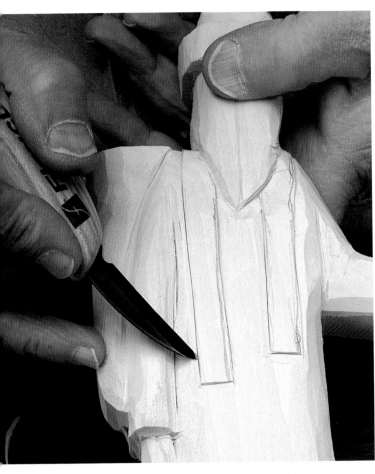

I have now cut away the excess wood from all around the scarf.

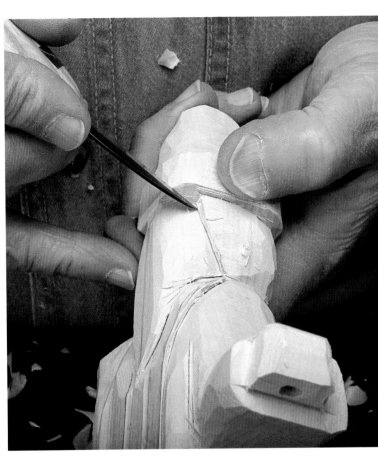

Now cut away to the beard and hairline on both sides of the head.

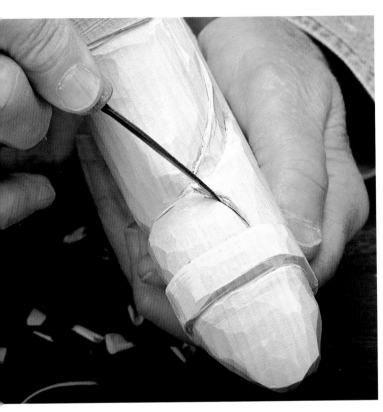

Draw in the line where the hair separates from the beard. Incise the line with your knife.

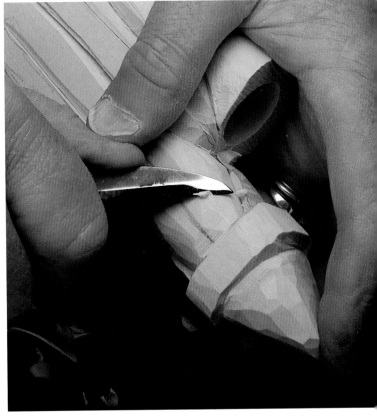

Begin rounding the head into the centerline.

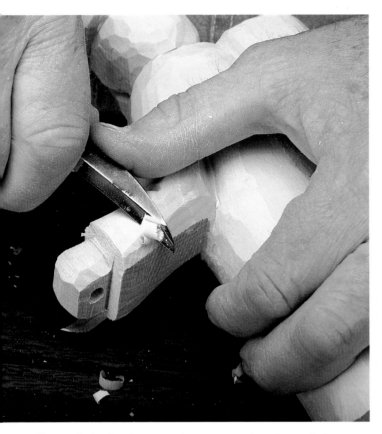

Shaping the body, taking away the waste wood on the arm before moving on to the details of the face and scarf.

I placed this hole in the top of the bag with a Forstner™ bit attached to a drill.

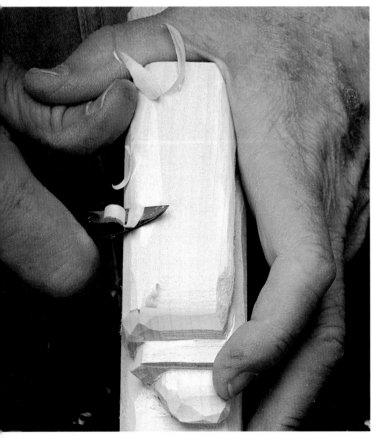

Shaping the bag. As you can see, I'm carving against the grain as I want to take a pretty good chunk off here.

Use your knife to round out the hole and make it bigger.

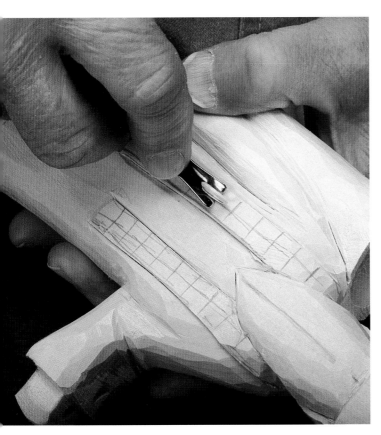

I'm putting the lines in the scarf for the checkerboard pattern with a V gouge.

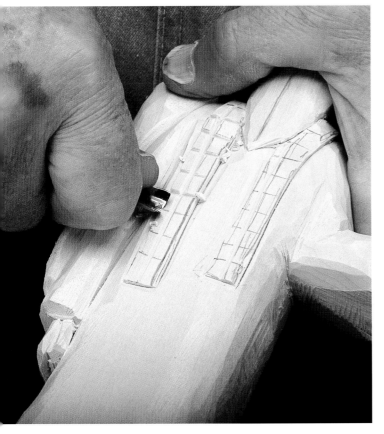

Make cuts horizontally and vertically on both sides of the scarf.

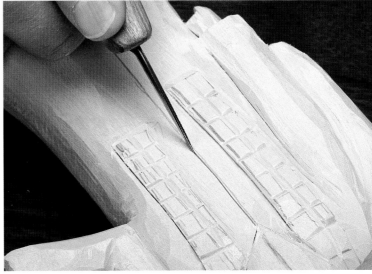

Incise the line down the front for the opening of Santa's robe.

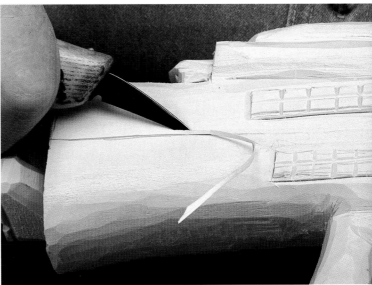

Take out the line of the robe, and the robe overlaps left to right … unless he's a "sissy."

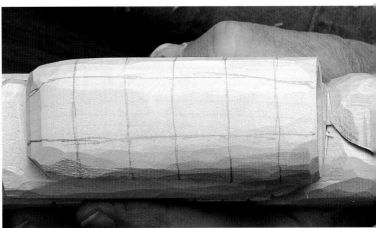

We've decided to make the bag a basket. I've drawn the lines on the basket.

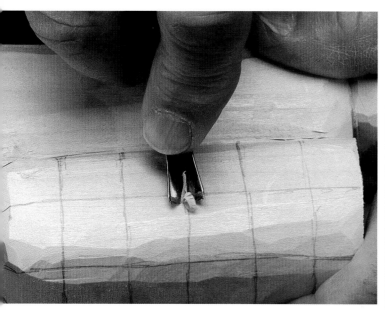

Take out the basket lines with the V gouge.

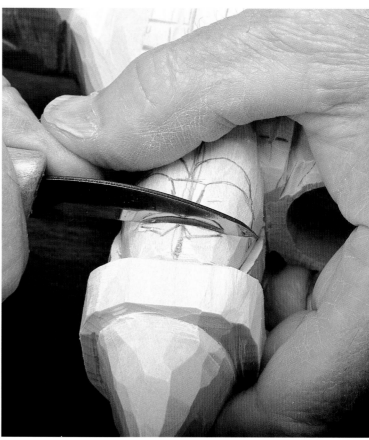

Incise along the eye channel.

The completed basket.

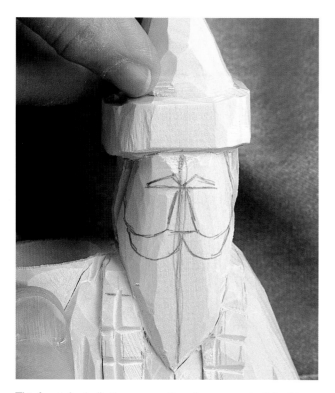

This face is basically the same as the others, except a little thinner.

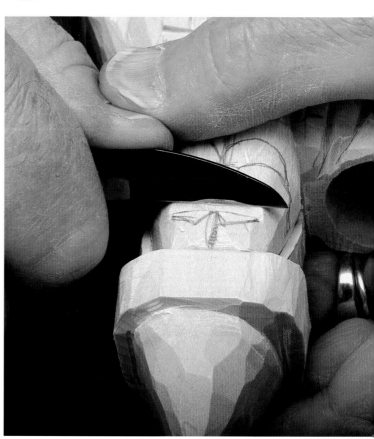

Cut a little angled piece out up to the incised eye channel line.

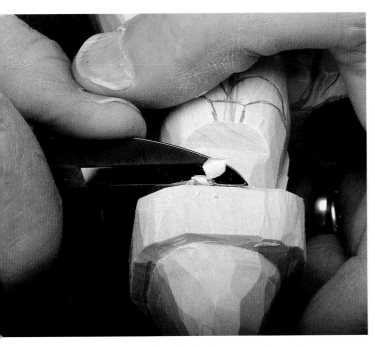

Cut away the excess wood on the forehead from the eyebrows up to the hat to give the nose more definition.

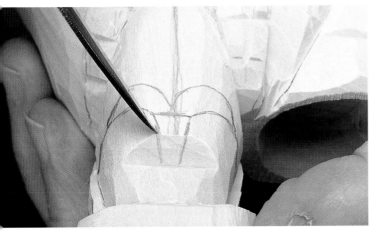

Draw the lines of the nose back in and incise around the nose.

Incise around the nose and cheeks.

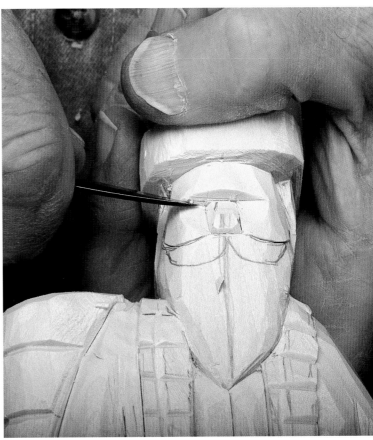

Begin cutting away from around the nose.

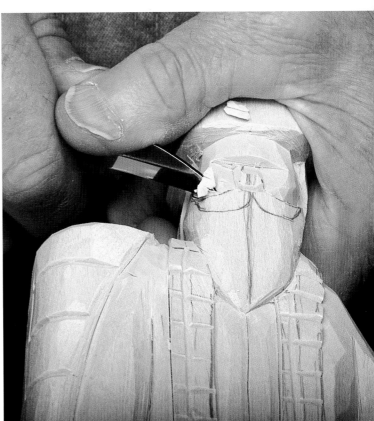

Round the cheeks into the mustache.

Carve out the details of the face. It is similar to the others. Now let's add the eyebrows and eyes.

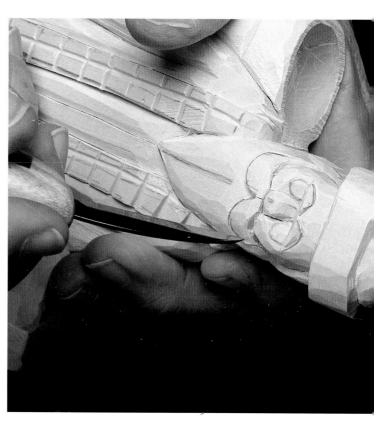

Because this Santa has a narrow face, I've made the eyes a little bigger and rounder to make them more prominent on the face.

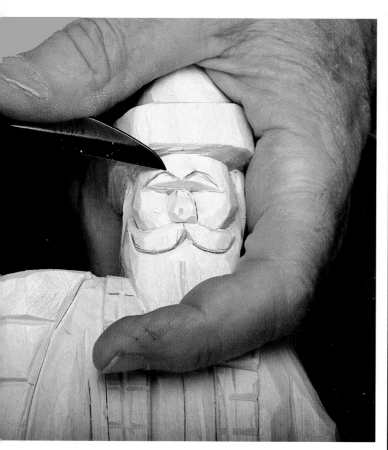

Carefully trim around the eyebrows. If you accidentally cut them off, you can always paint them on.

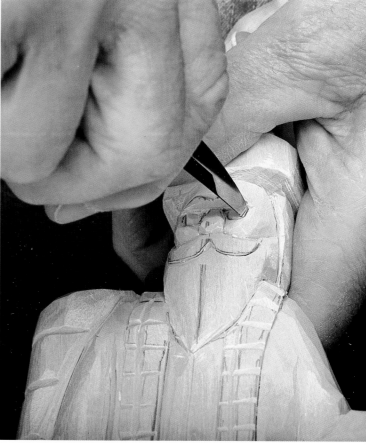

Remember to cut in deeply on each side of the eye with your knife.

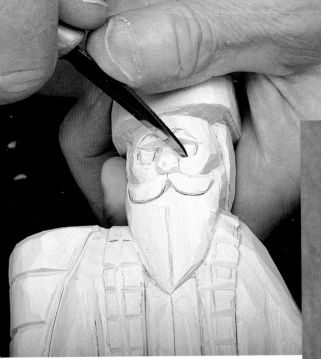

Come back and round the eye into the top of the cheek.

The difference in these two snow people is one has a top hat and the other a toboggan.

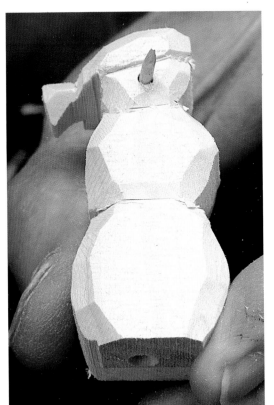

My snowman is just three little circles, carved smaller as they go up. Use your knife to round the edges down. Make it round. I don't know what to tell you except make it round! The carrot nose is a toothpick.

I'd like to say I carved the snowballs ... but I didn't. I bought them at a craft store. In the past I've drilled small holes in the bag and fastened little hearts or stars into the bag. Paint this Santa with Tompte red, Christmas Green, Black, White, Flesh Tone, and I've found an antiquing gel by Delta™. It is Dark Brown.

This is the same pattern with a little variation I've shown with dotted lines on the pattern. I've taken a little of the waste wood off again with the Foredom™ tool, which is a high-speed grinder.

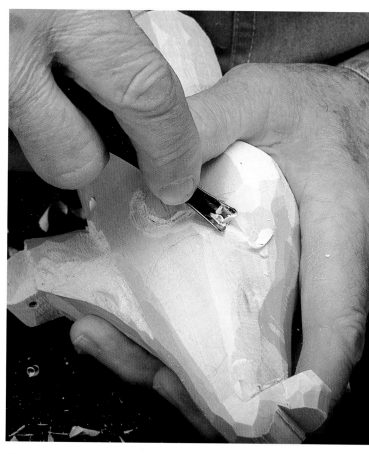

Use the gouge to get some definition around the arm.

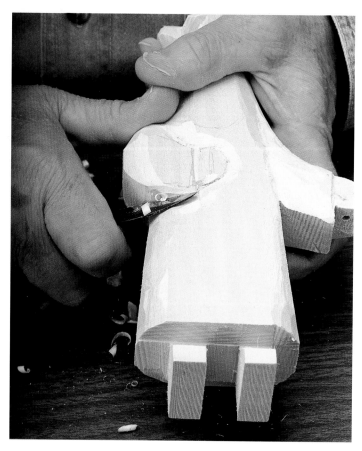

Start rounding.

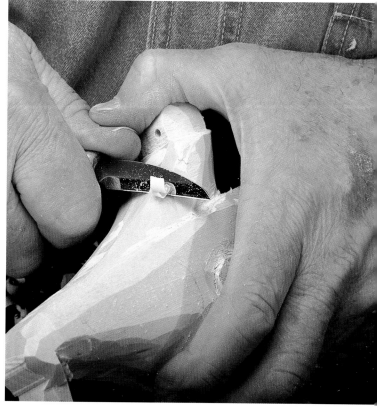

Working on the extended arm, you are cutting against the grain a bit and you need a good, sharp tool.

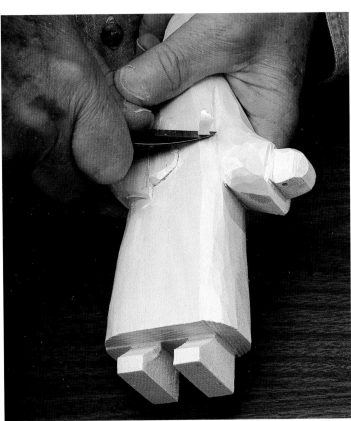

Speaking of sharp tools, I'm almost looking forward to sharpening tools now since I've found the Ultimate Honer™ from Chipping Away, Inc.™

Rounding down the body.

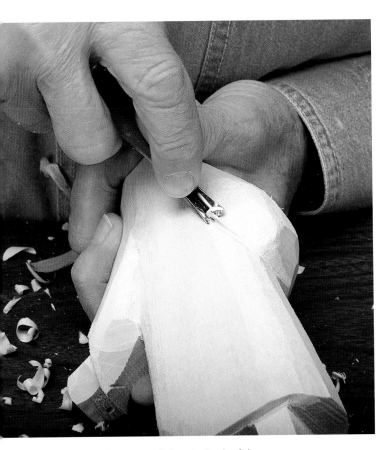

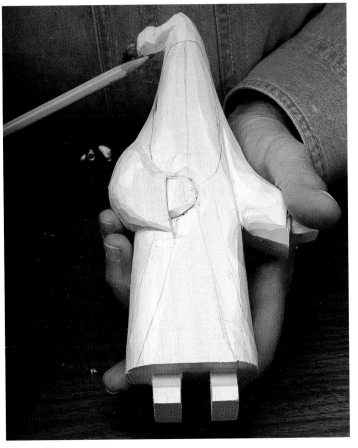

I'm using the V gouge to define the back of the arm.

I've drawn the centerline down the face, the outline of the face and beard, and the edges of the robe.

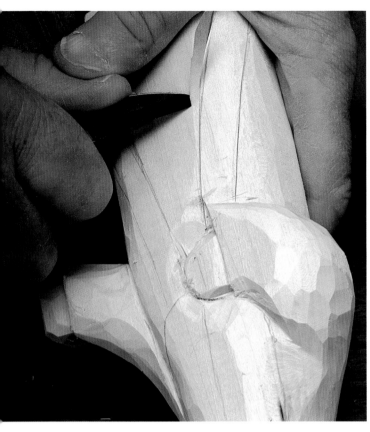

I've incised the line and am removing excess wood at an angle into the incised lines, raising the robe above the underlying garment.

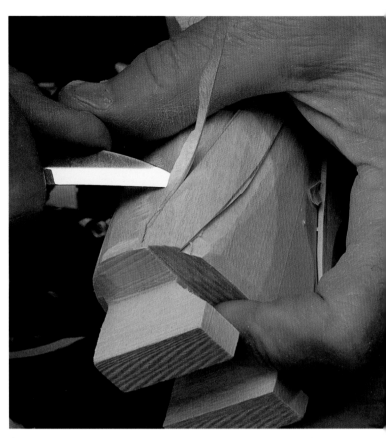

Cutting out along the other side of the star strip at the border of the robe, using the same technique as on the inside edge of the robe.

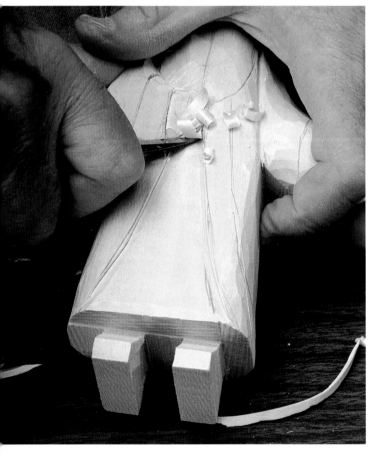

Continue to clean out where the inner and outer robe separate.

Repeat on the other side of the robe, raising the star strip border above the rest of the robe.

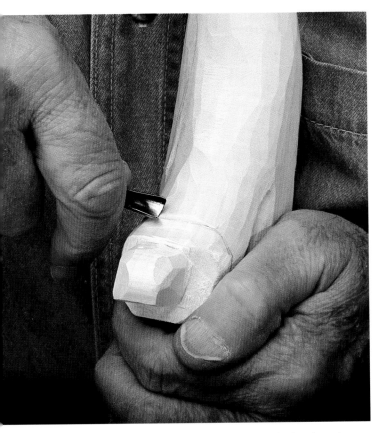

This time I've decided to use the V gouge to cut in the fur along the sleeve. Working against the grain here is made easier using the gouge.

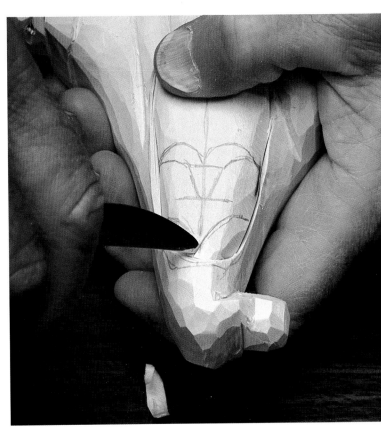

Just to show you something different, I'm adding hair to the forehead. I think his forehead was a little too long without it. Incise along the lines of the face.

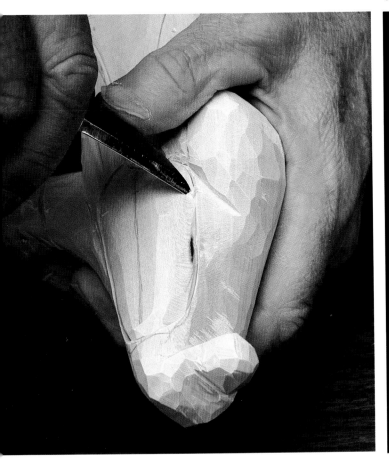

I've outlined the face as before.

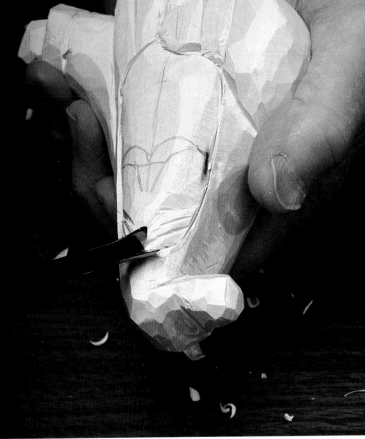

Add a few hair lines with the gouge.

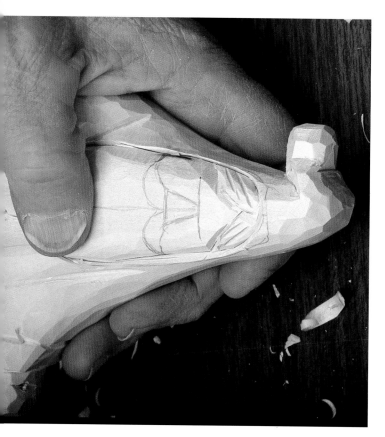

I've drawn the eye channel back in.

I've brought out a new set of interchangeable gouges for carving some details.

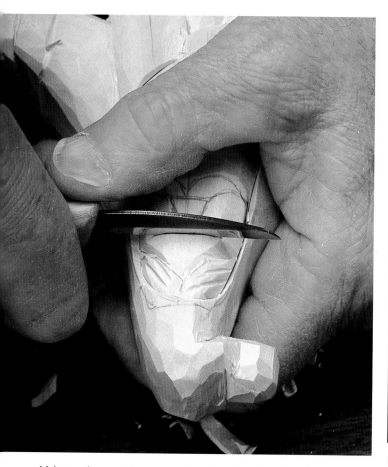

Making a deep rocking cut into the channel with this big old knife.

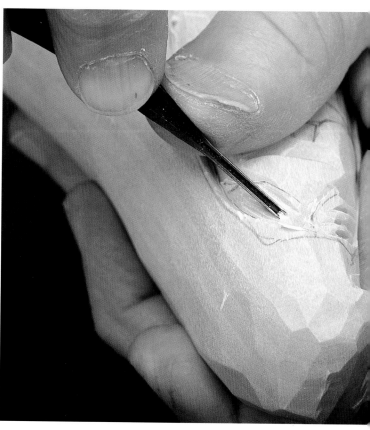

I've changed to the smaller gouge because I was not happy with the way the hair looked.

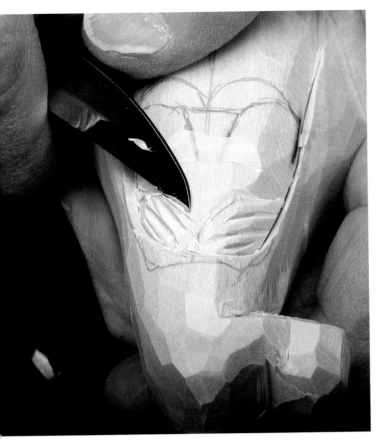

As with the other faces, I'm cutting away from the forehead to make the nose more prominent.

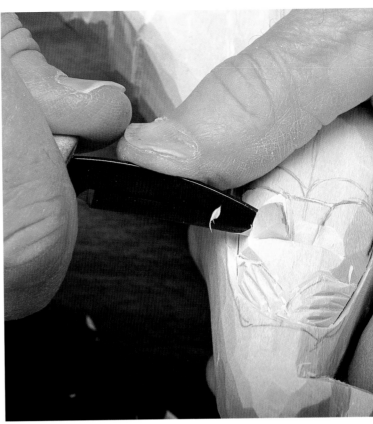

Taking a piece out next to the nose.

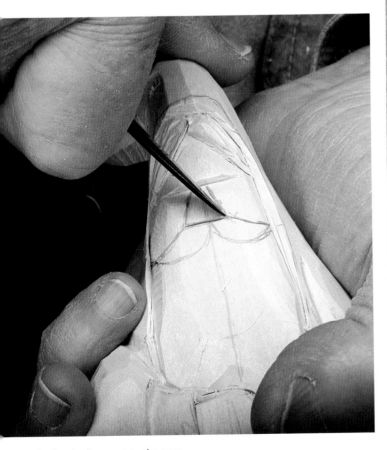

Incise the line next to the nose.

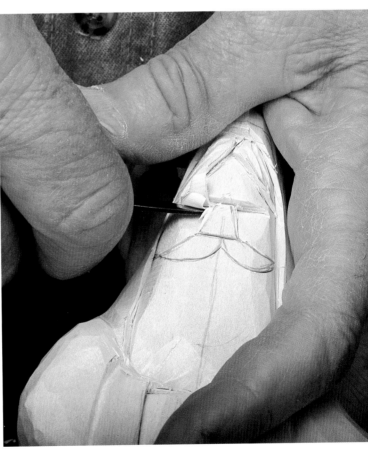

Continue to cut in around the nose until the nose is as prominent as you want.

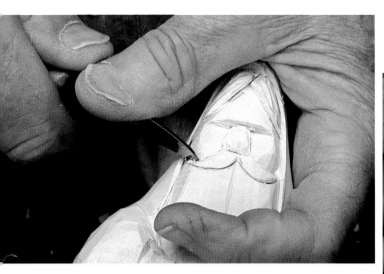

Round the cheeks again. Santa doesn't have a birthmark. This is just an imperfection in the wood.

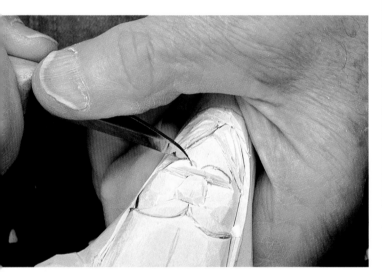

Cutting in the eyebrows.

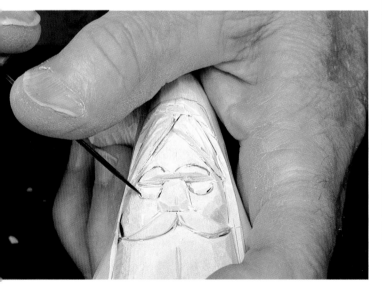

I've incised around each eye, cutting in deeply at the corners and rounding the eye into the cheek.

Adding some wrinkle lines at the bottom of Santa's outfit.

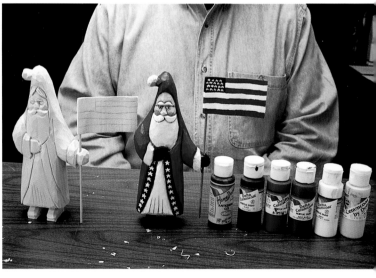

The flag can be painted like the American flag, but the number of stars is up to you as this is an old Santa. Do fifty if you like. The paints are Tompte Red, Navy Blue, Flesh Tone, White, Black, and Dark Brown antiquing gel by Delta™.

The Santa with a tree is a favorite with the Folk School. It is very traditional … and it looks a lot harder than it is!

At the bottom of the tree is a good place to use a gouge to remove excess wood.

We're going to put in this tree first. Incise just as deeply as you can go. If the knife comes out the other side that's okay (Ha!).

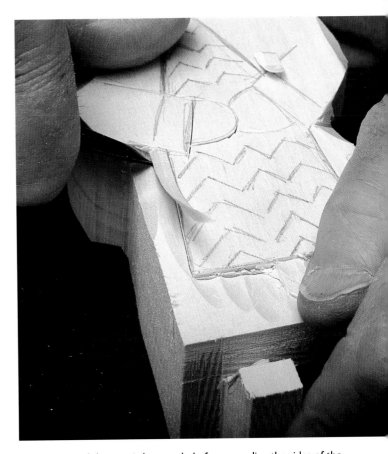

Cutting around the tree is best to do before rounding the sides of the figure. That way you know how much you have to cut.

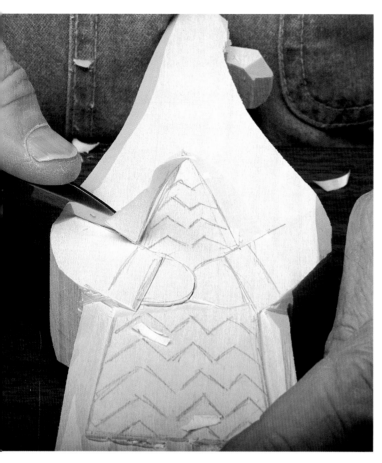

Continue up to the top of the tree.

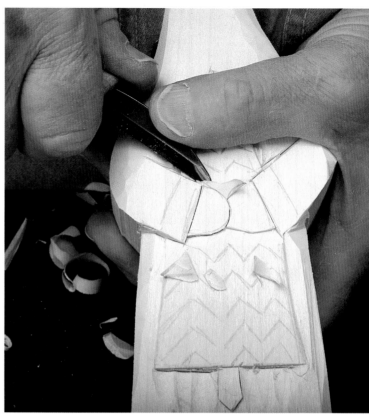

Trim around both hands.

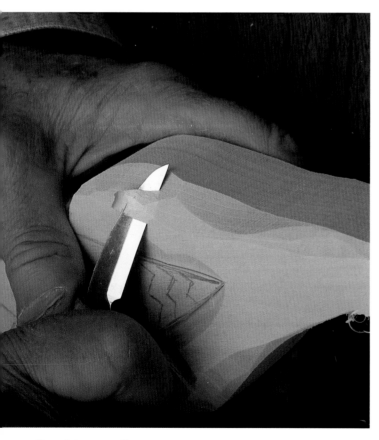

Round the arms off.

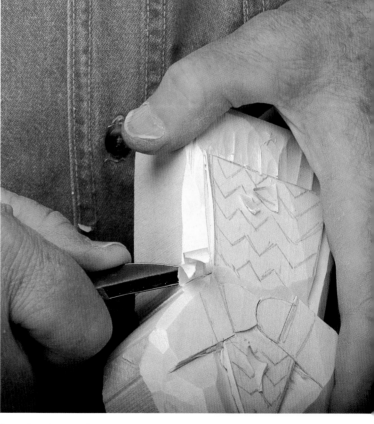

Round each side of the robe up to the tree.

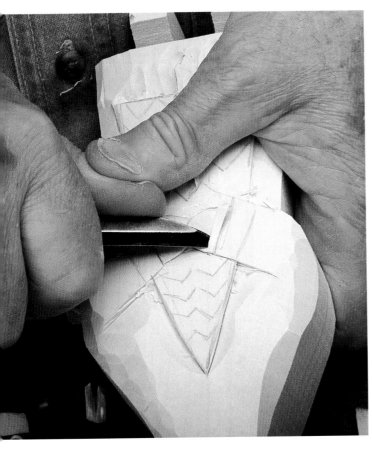

Remember, the gloves go into the sleeves.

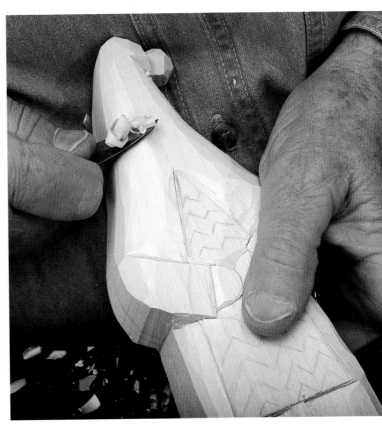

As usual, we're going to round the face area.

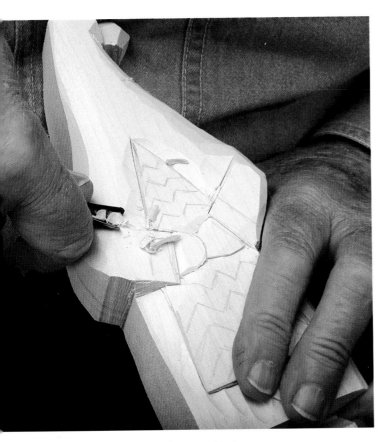

Adding a little definition to the arm with the gouge.

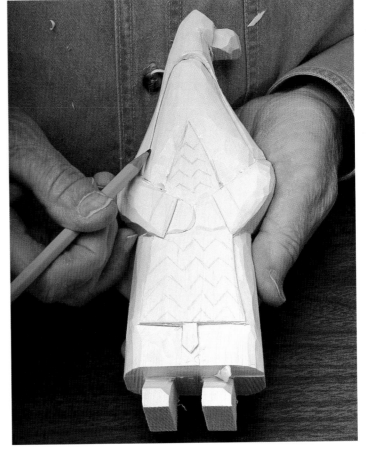

I made this Santa with a bigger face and beard on account of the tree.

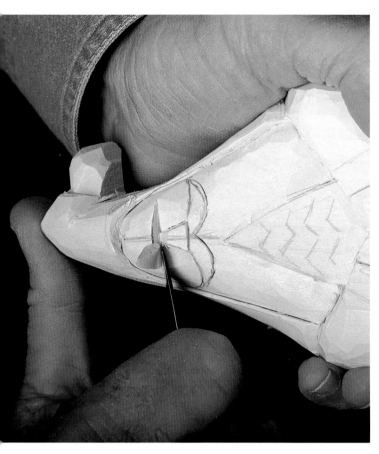

Remembering the other faces, incise along each side of the nose.

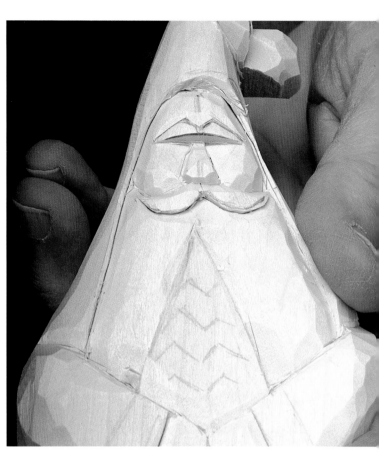

I've made all the cuts necessary for the face. The only difference here is the larger size of the beard to account for the tree in the middle.

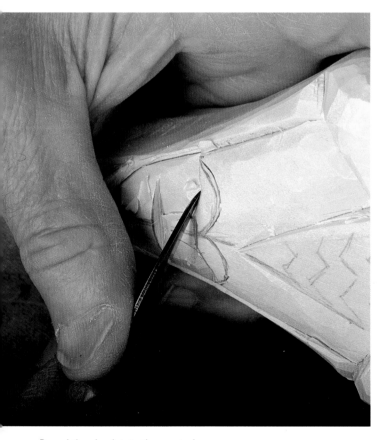

Round the cheek into the mustache.

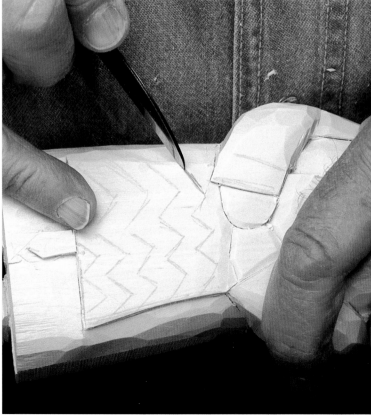

Incise each of the little jagged lines on the tree.

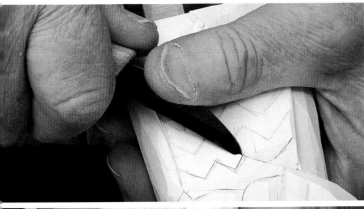

As you can see, the only difference is the tree with the special treatment. The paints used are Tompte Red (I use Tompte Red because it matches blood pretty well … and if people collect several of my Santas, they all have the same color.), Christmas Green, White, Black, Flesh Tone, Light Blue (for the eyes), and Dark Brown antiquing gel. Blend the Red and Flesh Tone to make the pink on the cheeks. Blend the pink into the cheeks, avoiding creating clownish dots.

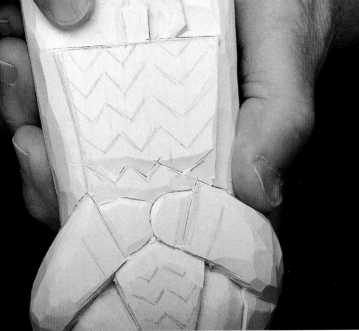

Then cut back at an angle and remove the chip. Repeat this process. Those of you who are into chip carving will enjoy doing this tree.

Here's the completed chip carved tree.

This is Santa with the Fish and the Cat.

Just round down the edges of this whimsical cat. It isn't supposed to look real.

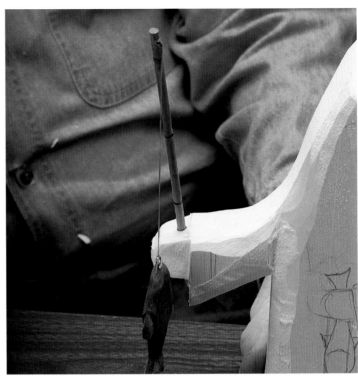

In the future I plan to angle the hole in the hand so the fish hangs better in front of Santa.

This is about as rounded as the cat needs to be. Santa's fishing pole is a dowel rod and the fishing line is 30-pound test dental floss.

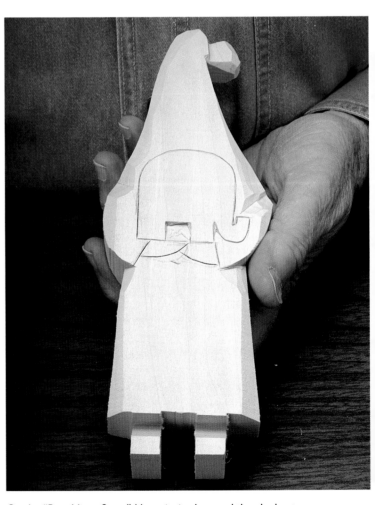

On the "Republican Santa" I have incised around the elephant.

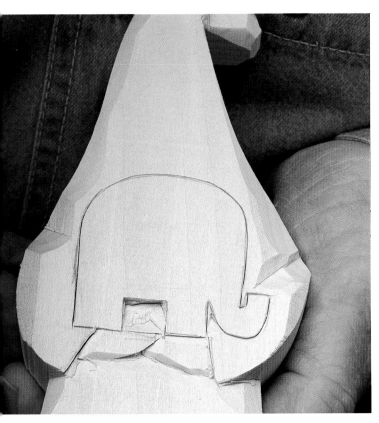

I've cut out around the hands now as well.

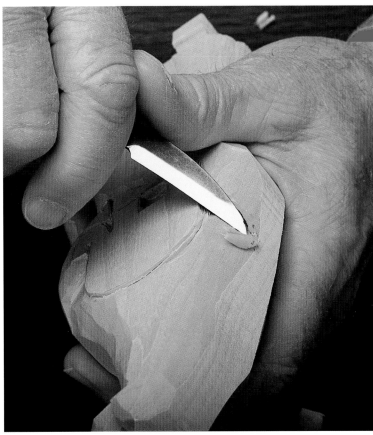

Rounding the arm to make the elephant figure more prominent.

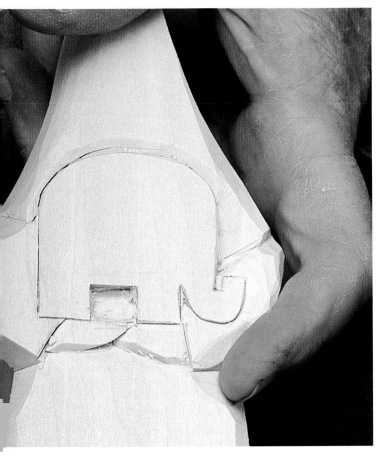

I've cut out around the elephant to make him stand out more.

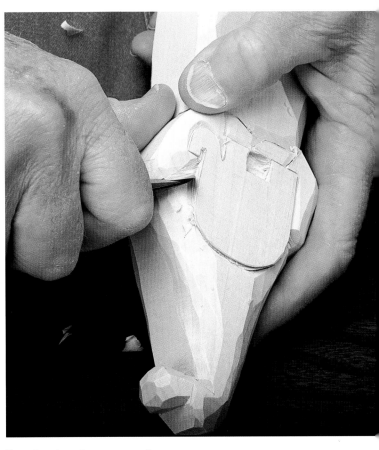

Rounding the other arm as well.

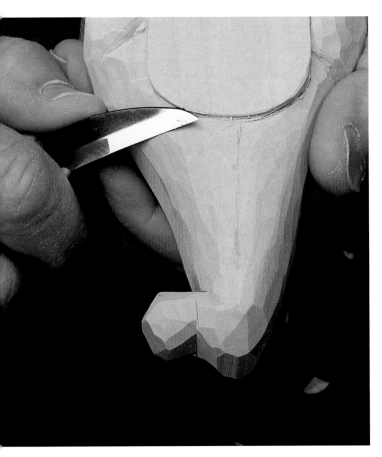

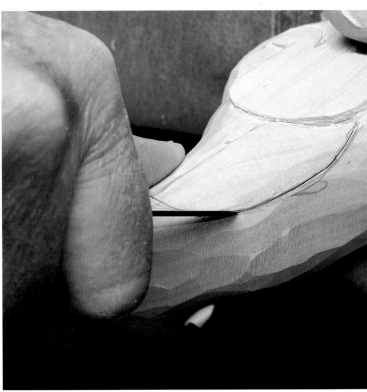

Deeply incise around the line for the face.

I'm starting to get the egg shape for the face and to round up to the centerline.

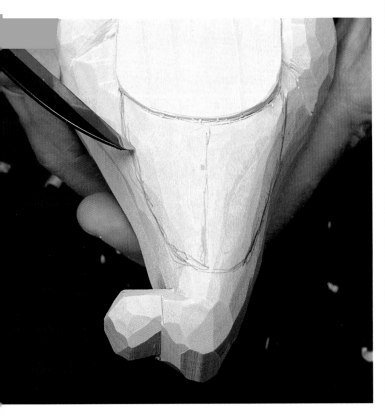

Draw in the outline for the face.

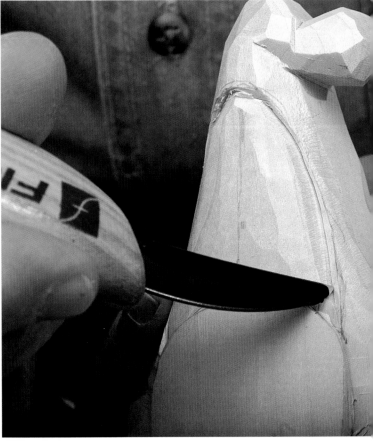

Cut away excess wood to make the face area prominent.

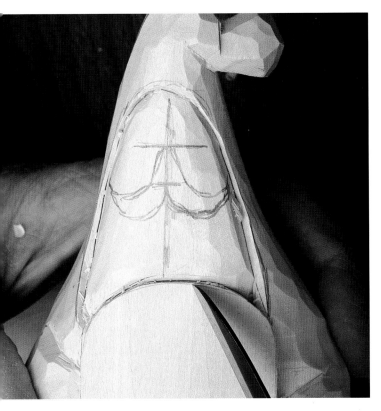

Draw in the face.

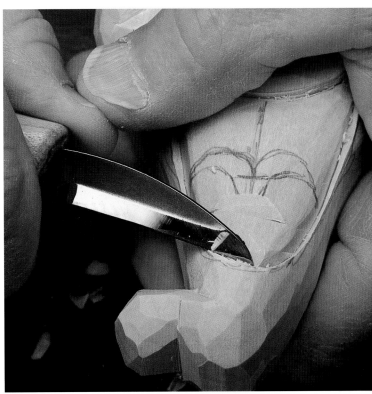

I've made the initial cuts, reducing the forehead to make the nose more prominent and adding the angled cut into the incised line under the eyebrows for the eyes.

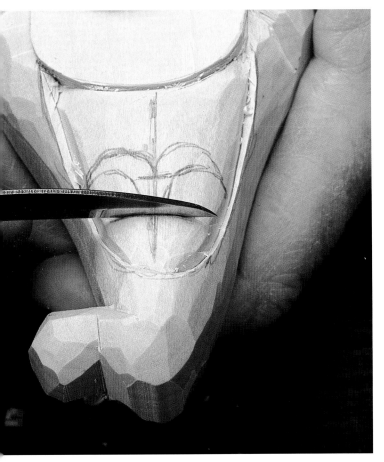

I'm starting the face carving again by deeply incising the eye line. The reason I repeat this is that people seem to have trouble with faces.

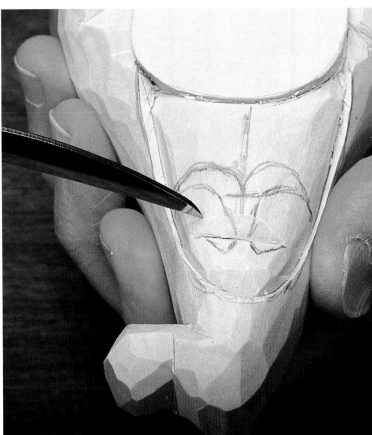

I've redrawn the nose and eyebrows. Even though we do the same process on each face, they all will look different.

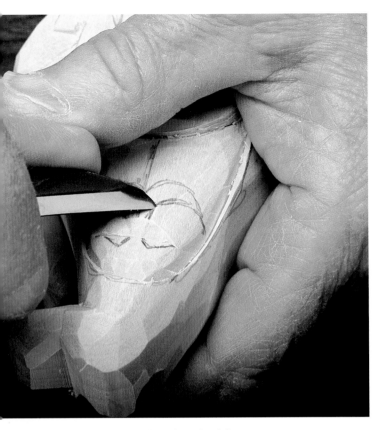

Angle the blade to cut along the side of the nose.

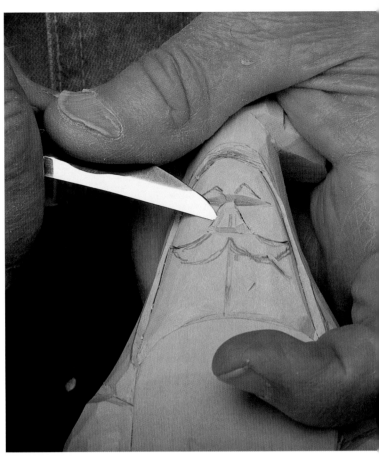

I've trimmed around the nose and am starting to round the cheeks.

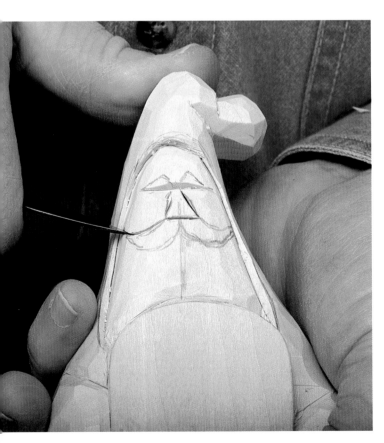

Do both sides of the nose and then incise the line between the cheek and mustache.

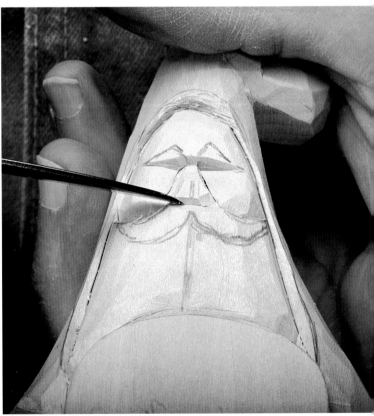

I've rounded the cheeks and cut a little notch under the nose.

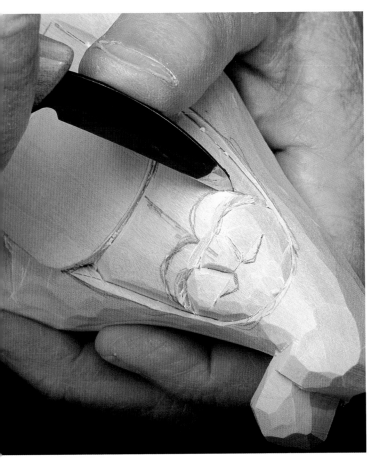

Incising around the mustache.

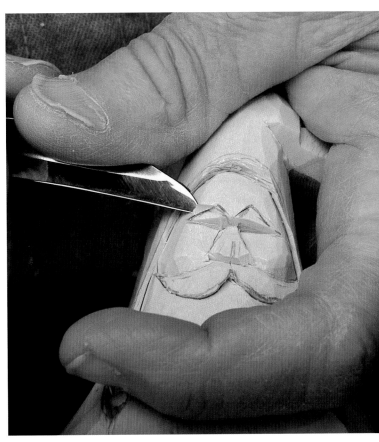

Carefully cutting around the eyebrows. In the class I've found that about as many eyebrows as balls are cut off. (Balls on the hood that is!)

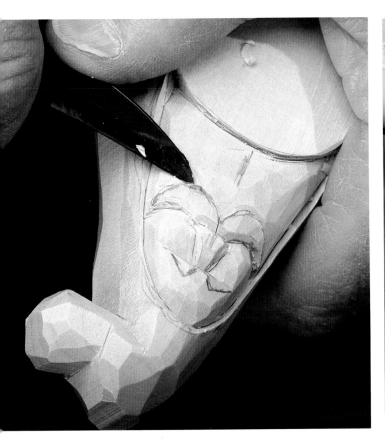

Removing the wood under the mustache with angled cuts.

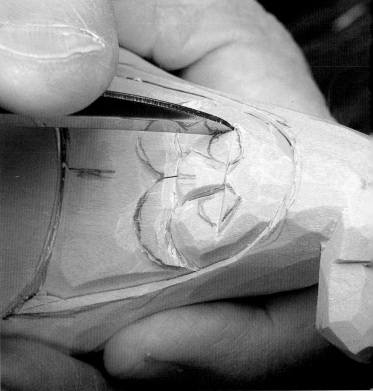

Remember to carve the eyes, incising deeply on either side and rounding the eyeball down into the cheek.

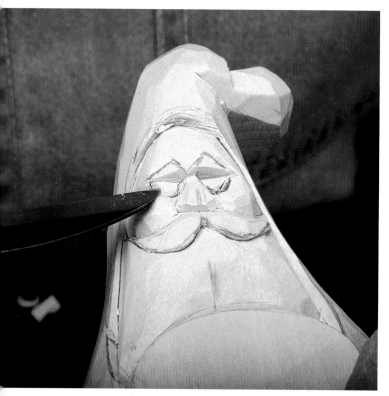

Rounding the eyeball.

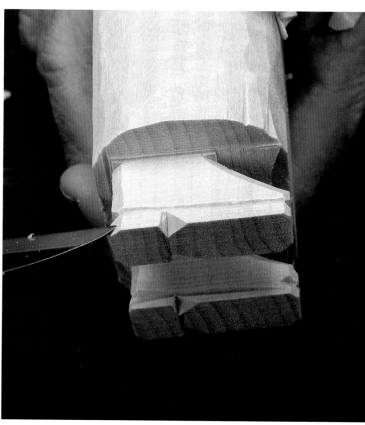

Don't forget to shape your shoes.

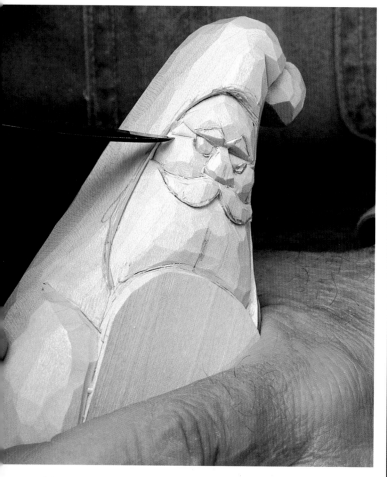

Add some laugh lines to make this Santa happy, which also indicates the many different styles possible starting with the same eyes.

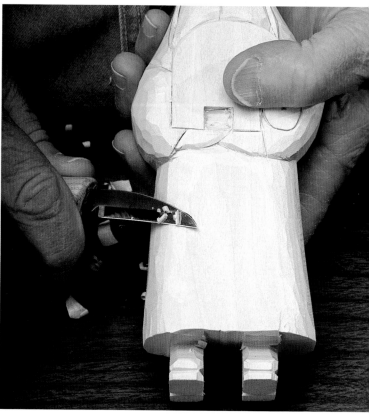

I've rounded the body and am getting ready to add the fur.

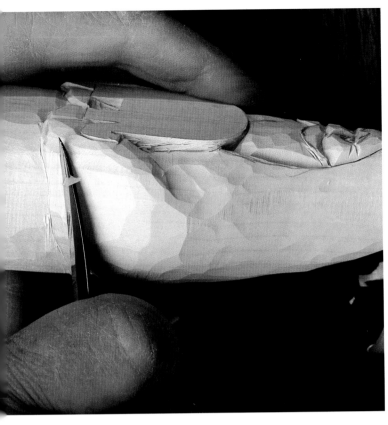

Remove saw marks or they will show up as rough spots when you paint.

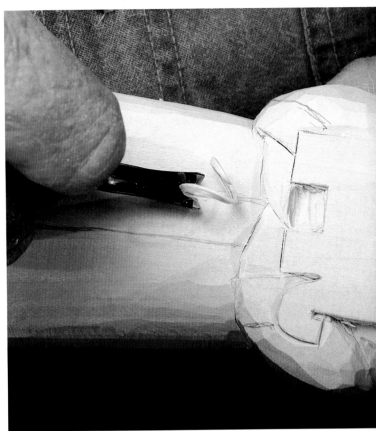

Outlining the fur with the gouge.

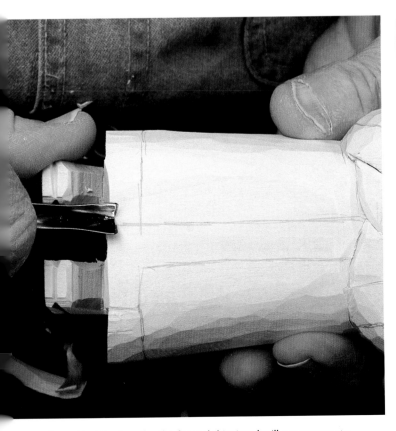

I've added the lines for the fur and this time I will use a gouge to outline the fur.

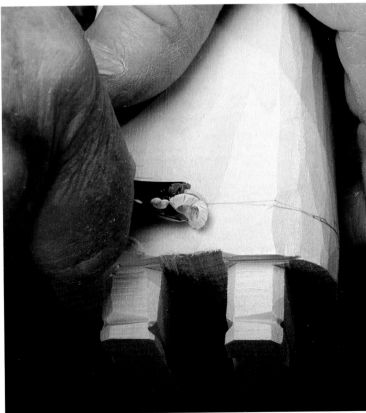

Continuing around the back.

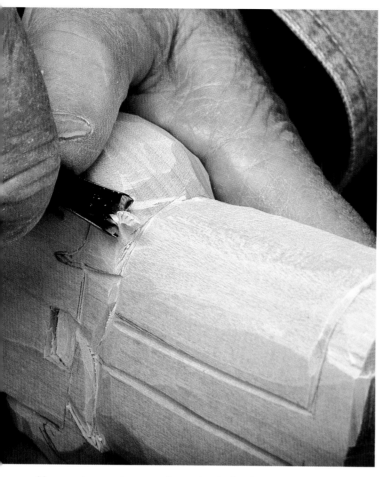

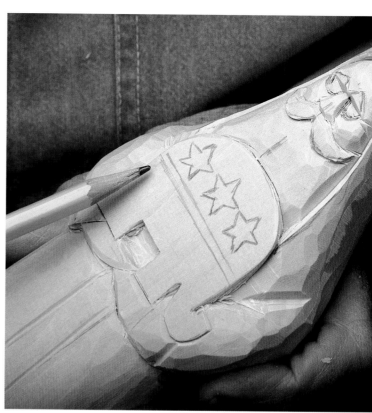

I've drawn in the stars. This Santa is ready to paint. If you're a Democrat, you can always use this Santa for target practice!

You can also use the gouge for cutting in the sleeve.

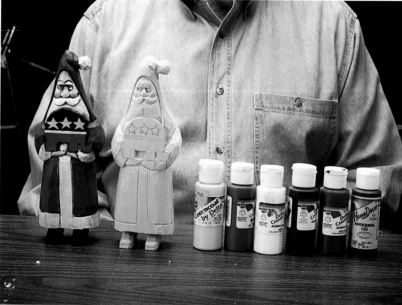

This Santa is painted with Tompte Red, Flesh Tone, Navy Blue, White, Black, and Dark Brown antiquing gel.

The sleeves and fur are cut in.

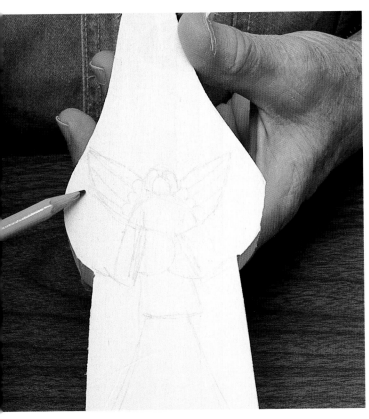

This is Santa holding an angel. As you are now all experts at Santa faces and such, I will only show you carving the angel.

I am relieving around the angel to get enough angel showing to put in a little detail.

I have incised around the angel, Santa's arms, and his hands.

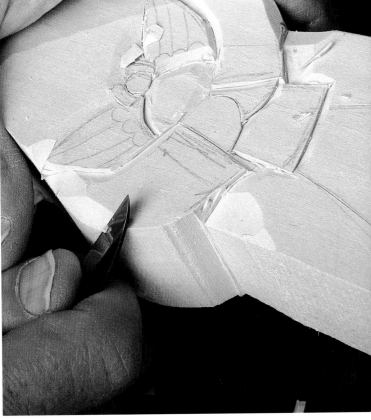

Round the shoulders so the wings will stick out.

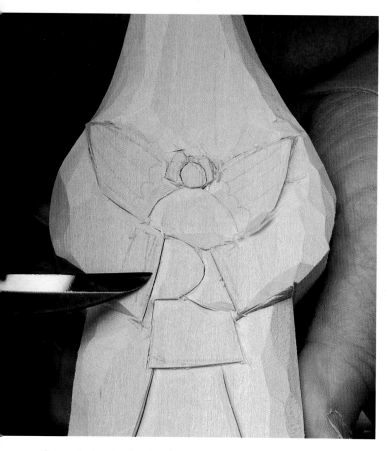

Shape the hands, showing them going into the sleeves.

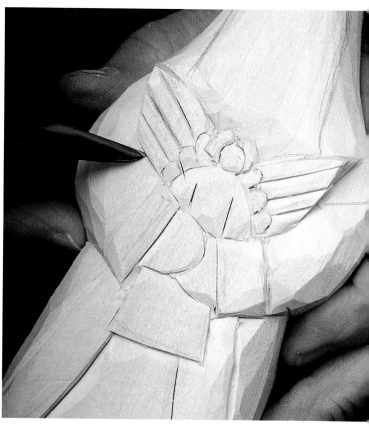

I've carved in the wings. This could easily be done with a wood burner, which I did on the painted piece we will show later.

I've continued to cut away from the angel and define it a little better.

Here is the Santa holding the angel painted. This is the same paint scheme as before, although you can use whatever colors you prefer on the angel's robe. The robe shown here is light blue. The angel's hair is brown.

Gallery

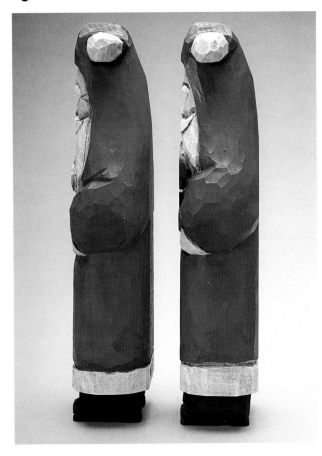

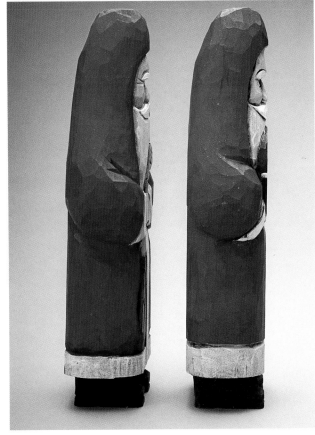

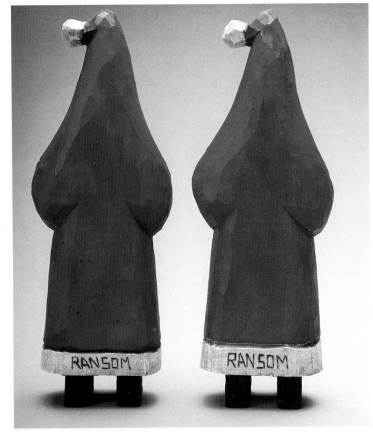

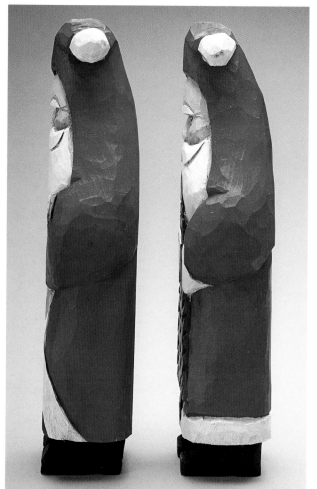

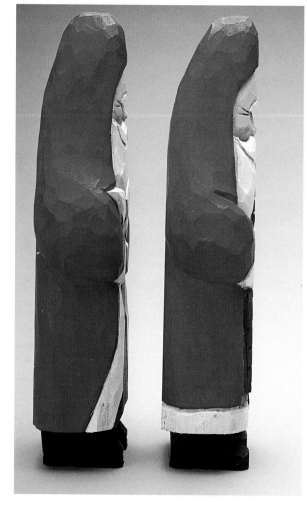

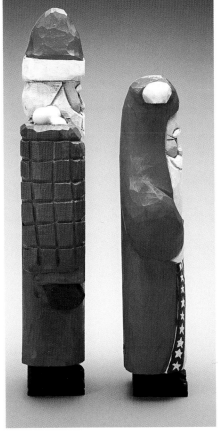

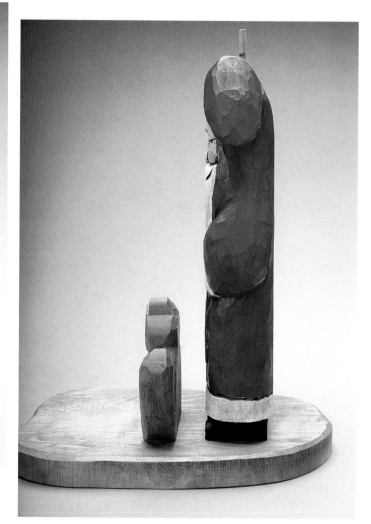